I0536979

Insight Out

Writing from the Center for Independence of the Disabled—New York

Fall 2011

NY Writers Coalition Press
Brooklyn—2011

Copyright © 2011 NY Writers Coalition Inc.

Upon publication, copyright to individual works returns to the authors.

ALL RIGHTS RESERVED

ISBN-13: 978-0-9787794-5-0

Editor: Avra Wing
Graphic Designer: Deborah Clearman

Insight Out contains writing by the members of the creative writing workshop conducted by NY Writers Coalition Inc. at CIDNY.

NY Writers Coalition thanks the following supporters, without whom this writing workshop and anthology would not exist: Kalliopeia Foundation, the NYC Department of Cultural Affairs, Two West Foundation, the WellMet Group, and all our individual donors and attendees of our annual Write-A-Thon.

NY Writers Coalition Inc. is a not-for-profit organization that provides free creative writing workshops throughout New York City for people from groups that have been historically deprived of voice in our society. For more information about NY Writers Coalition Inc.:

NY Writers Coalition Inc.
80 Hanson Place #603
Brooklyn, NY 11217
718-398-2883
info@nywriterscoalition.org
www.nywriterscoalition.org

The Center for Independence of the Disabled—New York's goal is to ensure full integration, independence and equal opportunity for all people with disabilities by removing barriers to the social, economic, cultural and civic life of the community.

CIDNY
841 Broadway #301
New York, NY 10003
212-674-2300
info@cidny.org
www.cidny.org

INSIGHT OUT

INTRODUCTION

Our workshop began in March of 2009 at the Center for the Independence of the Disabled in Manhattan. Sitting crammed in around the table in the tiny kitchen, we talked, laughed, ate and, most importantly, wrote. Even though all of us there had some kind of disability, our writing wasn't focused on that. Each week for two hours we were free to express ourselves simply as people. Our thoughts and feelings were what defined us, and they have no limitations.

Some members have been there from the very first meeting; others have joined more recently. We have graduated from the kitchen to a conference room (though we still nosh). Whatever the mix or venue, we each look forward to our sessions and to hearing the beautiful, funny, moving and profound words of the others.

Although most members did not see themselves in this way before the workshop started, each of them is now, in fact, a writer. I do not know a definition of writer other than someone who is committed to writing. That is true of everyone in our workshop.

The structure of our meetings is simple: I give the group

a prompt—a writing suggestion—and then I ask everyone to write in response to it if they want. The prompts can be anything from a line of poetry to an ad on Craig's list to a fortune cookie to an excerpt from a video game manual. No matter what the prompt is, I am always amazed at the varied and creative work it elicits.

What follows is a sample of some of the poems and stories written in our workshops during the last two years. We are pleased to be able to share them with you.

Avra Wing, Workshop Leader

THE CEREMONIAL MASK OF TERROR

He was lost in the jungle. Middle-aged, short, he bore a worn and haggard expression. The heat engulfed him, as did the strangling vines of the tropical trees. And the insects, oh, the swarm of buzzing, crawling, and biting little beasties hovered all about his strained form. The photo safari was gone. It had left him stranded, not thinking of searching for him in the hellish environment where he could in no way find his bearings. No broad avenue existed for a city fellow like him to stroll casually home. He would have to hack his way through the entangling mire.

However, alone and afraid, he had no machete nor energy to carve a path of his own. Then, through the blur of sweat that covered his eyes, he saw it, hideous and terrifying. The creature pounced upon him wrenching the breath from his lungs, toppling him to the wet jungle floor. The wretched beast, a skeletal form with intertwining scales, thrust its claws deep into the man's chest. The creature's fangs, dripping with slime, punctured his throat. The man, barely alive, screamed out in agony.

He remembers very little now. He wakes up in a dim haze of consciousness. He cannot move. He cannot hear. He cannot see. Now he only drifts in and out of a frail awareness, never knowing where he is, only knowing where he once has been. And this is all he knows. The world and life he had once been a part of is no more.

DOCTOR MARIGOLD

I'd like to be the doctor of this marigold—crumble it up and throw all the pieces away! However, there just might be some medicinal value to a crushed and crumbled marigold. It might enhance male sexual prowess for men over sixty—like me!

Should I take it raw by mouth or mix it with tea? It most likely would take a lot of crushed and crumbled medicinal marigold to get me all fired up again. Or would some scientist with a Ph.D. nurture these little jewels of health in vast quantities on some huge farm for a large pharmaceutical company that would process the secret essence of marigold into little yellow capsules and sell them for an exorbitantly marked-up price, far exceeding its cost to produce?

And will this Dr. Marigold, considering his financial ties to his pharmaceutical benefactors and motivated by corporate and personal greed, doctor his marigold miracle by diluting its formula by substituting daisies and ragweed, and thus turning this gift of renewed vitality into a dud for this old stud?

A DWELLING IN DISGUISE

The room was bare, just the confines of four walls. There was a door to this space, a rectangular slab; a knob protruded meekly at one edge. Adjacent to the wall where hung the door, a wall exuded a window, lodged squarely amid the center. A trickle of daylight streamed inside. A drab curtain obscured the window's rim and partially closed casement and fully closed screen. The other two walls served to seal up the place, inhibiting movement beyond this peculiar domain. For there were two occupants dwelling in an odd fashion.

They each sat quite stiffly facing one another, each sitting in a rocking chair on either side of the window. One moment one stared out the window and then towards the wall. Finally, with a slow and cautious revolving of their heads they came to face one another. The woman wore no make-up, her hair still in curlers for years gone by. She wore a tattered robe and slippers. The man, who caught sight of her, was clothed in faded pajamas, his face gaunt and his hair a mess. His feet were bare.

"What are we going to do today?" the man asked.

"There is nothing that we haven't done before," the woman replied.

"It's so sad, too much of a bore," said the man.

"I don't know what we can do. Do you think there's

anything new?" the woman responded with a glint of enthusiasm in her shrill voice.

The man forced a slim grin. "We can gamble like yesterday, or we can grumble in some other way."

"My head is hot," the woman expounded, one of her boney fingers scarcely skimming her forehead.

"My feet are cold," the man countered, rubbing his bare feet together, expecting the friction to work some wonder.

"Let's go fishing," he blurted out unexpectedly.

"I don't like fishing. I don't like fish."

"Why don't we watch TV?"

"Because we have no TV," she said.

"We're locked in here always just rocking back and forth looking at each other," finally mused the man. "We're always looking at each other," he went on.

"We're looking too long at each other."

"Let's do something new."

"We've been sitting here for days."

"No, I think weeks, or months, or maybe years. I can't be sure."

The woman rocked back and forth in the chair. "We're just sitting in these chairs. I wonder if we'll just continue to rock all day?"

"Maybe all night too, just as always."

"It's so sad to say or even to think. Yet I need my sleep."

"How about we stop this and start again tomorrow? It couldn't be any worse."

"Yes. And then we could decide, agree on something we want to do," urged the man.

"But can't do," the woman sighed.

"It seems that way."

"Well, good night."

"Good night. And here's looking forward to another boring day tomorrow."

The doorknob jiggled as if someone was trying to get inside, but neither of them paid any attention. They both were drifting off to sleep.

SELFISH, TIFFANY, KITCHEN, KINDERGARTEN TEACHER

She is like the eggs in the bowl, broken and scrambled. I'm mixing them all up. I don't like Miss Tiffany, my kindergarten teacher. I don't like school. I can't play with my knife. I can't play on the swings. No, Miss Tiffany says come indoors. Be a little child and play by the rules, her rules.

I don't like Miss Tiffany's nagging and crabbing. When I'm at home I mix up my eggs and pour them into the pan. The heat is on high. Julia Child did it that way on TV the other day. But where's the butter? Here's the butter. But I didn't put the butter in the pan!

I don't want to take a nap now that it's 3:00. The other kids have their heads down on the table, but no, not me! Miss Tiffany is watching. She's looking away now. I stick out my tongue at her. I think school is a bore to sit inside for hours when I can be playing outside by myself, playing with my knife.

The eggs are burnt. The heat was too high. The eggs are sticking to the pan. My day is ruined. Miss Tiffany doesn't like me. She orders me around, and Julia Child can't cook eggs for beans.

I'm Not Disabled, I'm a Hippie

I like hippies. When I was younger
Poppy used to call me a hippie.
"She's a hippie," he would say a bit upset.
I wrote a poem about hippies.
"Don't worry, Mommy. The good people,
the hippies, will help us."
In the world there are phantoms, strangers.
Hippies are angels. Her name is Angela.
Often hippies are struggling about
who can take on an oppressor's voice.
My hippie, Wayne, was color blind.
He even did not see my disability,
just my soul.

POPPY

I want to make a sculpture of Poppy's hands.
His hands had a history.

We loved avocados.
They are gold, avocados.
Grandma had an avocado tree.

Poppy, though not innocent,
Took care of our garden
As if he was a child.
His plants were his luxury.
Poppy was a man-child.
His plants saved his soul.

MEMORY

My memory is hidden from me.
For this reason
I am blind.
My ghosts don't let me be.
They taunt me because
my memory of them
is like the
glass menagerie
miniatures of glass
within my
dreams.

GO PLACES IN MY LIFE

I was on the run most of my life.
Need was not the necessity, but for the sake of freedom.
My Italian doctor practiced untraditional methods of medicine.
I was terrified of my family. They were sweet and humble.
But my disability makes enemies.
Some of the methods of my Italian doctor were a ritual.
He would go on vacation for the month of August. He left me
to my own devices. It was a free spirit
that he cultivated within me.

KEEP SMILING

Sometimes I see blind people. They have an apparent
disability. My disability is hidden. Sometimes my inability
to see my disability makes me confused.
People with physical disabilities seem to have a lifestyle
that the world accommodates. If you have a hidden disability
the world does not see you.
Sometimes people with disabilities are deaf to emotion.
Unable to see their disability. At times they create one
so the world may see.
My disability now is my smile.
It's sad. But now the world sees me.

FACES

Faces, faces, faces
I don't see my face
Self-portrait of illusion
In my life I see many walking phantoms
Faces, faces, faces
The image in the mirror is invisible
Self-portraits of illusion
Seen too many
Faces become phantoms
Faces, faces, faces
Photos tell me lies
And for this reason
I often cry
Faces, faces, faces
In the circus of life
I've seen many clowns
That don't wear makeup

Bagels

Wayne's specialty was making poverty food
into gourmet dreams.
He watched cooking shows on Channel 13.
Channel 13 about American life.
Sewing programs, music programs.
Day-old bagel could be saved for a couple of meals.
Recipe was a little bit of Mrs. Dash,
onion, mayonnaise and melted cheese.
We were poor but not desperate.
In his memory I want to write poetry about bagels.
I dream about bagels.

Peso de Vida

My writing is almost
an unburdening to the ocean.
I write and I offer
Peso de Vida.
My life was a burden.
I survived by running.

ASHES, ASHES

Maybe my poems are precious to me
because they too will belong to nature.
Teacher, please teach me to love my poems
because in my heart they found a home.

Poppy died.
Mrs. C died.
Dr. Umpierre died.
Wayne died.

Maybe my poems are a way
of talking to the dead.
The poems are my soul's safety.

Ashes frighten me.
I smoke because my life
is filled with ashes.

THE CHILD I CAME FROM

I am from that school in Los Angeles for handicapped children—the first of its kind—where 40 children packed the first grade, and Zada, the teacher, got them to get out of their wheelchairs and under their wooden desks during an air raid drill so that they would be ready for an imminent nuclear attack.

I am from that home for mentally-challenged children where I first saw myself in "their" eyes—a child who couldn't read or write and who walked around with her mouth open in awe of what she saw.

I am from that recurring nightmare where Pinocchio with his long wooden nose laughs at me from a deserted island while I float away in a dark sea until his image fades and I wake up screaming.

I am from those hurtful words that burned in my mind—words so cruel that I did everything I could to make them not true until—as a young woman—people apologized for their thoughts of me.

I am from New York City—a place where I can be all that I want to be—no longer worried about being fragmented and isolated and lonely.

And, finally, I am from my daughter, who is all that I would have hoped to be—a beautiful person inside and out—who shares her beauty with all those who listen.

LIGHT ON RIVER WATER

Light streaming on water has a pattern, and I am mesmerized by the river on this warm, reflecting day. My thoughts have lost their way, for they are careless of their journey. These thoughts have no place here, where the light nurtures me to healing.

CIRCUS DAYS AND NIGHT OWLS

Circus dogs bark to the heartbeat of the night owl. The time is the morning mist and the dawning of the light. The smell is the fresh vapor air. The touch is the early morning wind faintly passing. The dogs' master calls out, breaking the dance of the dogs' barking and the night owl's heartbeat.

A CERTAIN SLANT OF LIGHT

In a certain slant of light I see that you are the offspring of many continents. The light from that angle is a mirror of your past, which you can only glimpse at but never understand. You are the embodiment of all that has come before, and you are the maker of all that will come after.

HEROIC WOMEN

She looks tired every time I see her around six in the evening, sandwiched between all the others who are coming from work. I know what she does, and I know that she is like so many women in this city.

She looks like the world was taken out of her—her head dropping as the bus stops to pick up more passengers this Friday evening after work. There is nothing unusual about her looks—she looks ordinary—except that I know that she is an extraordinary person and that is why she looks so beaten up.

I know her because she is like so many who advocate on behalf of those who have such enormous needs that it is nearly impossible for one person to meet them. Yet I know she spends all her dying energy fighting for their cause without a thought for her own needs and desires.

I can tell from looking at her that she has had her energy drained from her this week. She appears to have only the strength to drag her body up the stairs and into her bed.

I know that she will probably sleep only three hours and be up Saturday morning to begin her plight all over again.

We ask a lot from some women, and they

shoulder their responsibilities with all the heroism of a soldier who goes into battle without complaint. They—these women—are the moral fabric of a society working for health care, housing, education and the psychological welfare of us all.

THE ROPE CHAIR

My master made me for the purpose of sitting in a modern art museum. My master made me to be aesthetic—that's why humans continually come to look at me Tuesday through Sunday all year round. They are intrigued by the rope that surrounds my spirit.

THE WRONG GALLERY

It was an unassuming door built to withstand the elements. The most curious aspect of the door was the lettering that was engraved into the glass. From the street I could see that it read: "The Wrong Gallery." On closer examination, I saw that there was no lock. The final shock came when I attempted to peer through the door only to see a white wall nearly touching the glass. Then I noticed a small tag to the right. I picked it up and squinted in an attempt to read the very small lettering. It said: "If you are looking for works of art, go elsewhere." I rang the bell on the left and entered the tiny room. The wall turned, and I found myself in a beautiful garden.

WANDERING

She sat a long time on the park bench, her mind wandering from one memory to another. Fleeting, never wincing, because they were like a movie reel that had been spliced up so badly the story had no meaning anymore. Then, after she settled on a memory—an old pair of jeans—she got up and began to walk toward the bathroom in Central Park. She walked there mechanically, threw open the door, took down her pants, plopped down on the toilet seat without looking, and peed. Then she got up, pulled up her pants and walked back out. She started walking toward the water, and when she got there she looked down and her mind started to wander again. The memories raced. None of them were good. They were all bad, but she never focused on any one of them. Suddenly, she saw an orange fish and she began to watch him, and then she remembered a time when she used to watch the fish in the park as a child.

WHERE IS THE LIGHT?

The animals know where the light is and where it is not.
It's not in the darkness of Halloween, Friday the Thirteenth
or Freddie Krueger. I don't know where the light is.
Maybe it's in the mind of women, but not men.
Men live in the dark side of caverns, of catacombs
where unspeakable things happen on the altar of holiness
in rooms that look sacred.
Cry out and cry out. Why are we meek
when sounds are silence and silence is sound?
Where are the animals, where is the light?
Is the day the night and the night the day? The day
is the world going to or moving away from itself.
The Virgin came to see me as she cried invisible tears
in the millennium of years.
Pray for the future. The future of life.
And ask the animals to see the light.

SUBURBIA

Suburbia is dead, murdered by the fire green as grass.
Let's move away from the purity of virginity and see
the rage of revealment. After all, Jack Kerouac and
Allen Ginsberg did it, so why can't we? But wait. There is no we
there's only I, you and me walking down the dark street
of life like a Mickey Spillane novel
where his words leap off the page as he breaks the bones
of those who are walking into the path of destiny.
But now the light is rising, coming over the coffee shops of life
where dreams come true, where the customers live with plans
for the shut-ins and toys for the orphan children.
Mickey's there, too, helping the little old ladies cross the street.

I'm wondering who I am and where suburbia is.
It seems to be afflicted, not seeing itself
sitting on the shelf of memory.
Life seems to be so restricted unable to breathe ready
to heave itself into oblivion but don't take me with you.
I still want to live and so many unspoken words.
The virus of the silent age ready to unmask itself
into its utterance of enlightenment
the new age of the beginning.
Can you see me are we still here?

The Adventure of My Life

The adventure of my life was never that nice. Dreams of travel to other places. The internalization of romantic spaces. The discovery of myself while being with someone else.

Yes, I would never take a plane or the train or the bus because I'd have to rush. I always wanted to fly, but would I have to say goodbye? Separations, the opposite of integration. Family, friends, the beginning without end. No need to pretend that my life was ahead of me and not moving toward my past.

Where is that physical investigation, spatial teleportation? Can you hear silence? The dead souls are weeping but no one is grieving. Some men are monsters, but all men are human in the eyes of humanity. Past their power and control a political goal. There will be no trouble to you because life is a final disintegration. It just depends on the time and type of transportation. A life is a romance if we have the choice. Take me there if you have the time, the day before nine.

Spring is the internalization of a romantic inquiry of the heart joining together while living apart.

THE RESURRECTION

I've always loved the 1960s, not just because of what it was, but because of what it meant.

His Voice—his music always made me feel like I was seeing pictures in sound. I always felt optimistic—full of hope like I was hearing music from a future being—this musical prophet of the Civil Rights Movement. Can you hear me, John? I can't see you but I know you're here. Your turmoil and your pain is a melodic and modal refrain uniting people in a global universe. Will you be there for the second resurrection? I know you must have hated heroin, but your music gives the world its next injection of love through sound. When you come, we'll all go up and meet the One. On the path of Love, the world will play and say hello, and not goodbye. It was a love supreme. The resurrection has begun. The long night is over and the angels are here. The collective sound where love and God are smiling because you were born.

The Exhibition

I want you to see this before I leave. The arbitration was held because the life was shelved. The premature contraction life's indiscriminate reaction. The permanent communication. Life is a temporary treasure in between forever. An invisible description only perceived from behind the screen of metaphysical life knocking on the door of reality.

I want you to see what can't be shown, all the things time moves toward the unknown, a life in itself. The metaphysical self. Between who I am and who I used to be. Is life the vibration trapped in the unknown? The gallery is fading, mourning the life that was. The exhibition is the abstract of contrition, penance given for the entrance that will never come. Who will forgive the one who didn't live? All the suicides are weeping, caught in the memories of their speaking. Touch the exhibition as if to touch my hand and bless my life. I want you to see what I've kept behind the screen before we meet again. Happy I could say these words on the page before the age of internalization. When the time leaves its mark on the reality of life. If you can see me hold on to the memory of yourself. Before you leave remember to be.

SEE YOU SOON, NEW FRIEND

Staring me in the face are new possibilities. Every day is a new adventure: a chance to succeed. A new day to forgive a misdeed. A new opportunity to meet someone different. A chance to go someplace I haven't been before. Or, once in a while, to make a fresh start, perhaps to learn to sing or play an instrument. Perhaps I will encounter a new store. Or give a gift, or receive one. Sadly sometimes to say goodbye to an old friend moving to a new location. Or to a loved one getting too old or ill to remain.

The beginning of a new day is always an adventure. A start. A look forward. A bright beginning. The ending of each day makes me a little sad. Luckily there is hope for a new tomorrow, with its large future.

I like to get mail, especially from friends and relatives. That's why I write them. Receiving news from people I love is fun. Getting up in the morning and hoping for a surprise letter or phone call is sweet.

I wonder what tomorrow will bring. Maybe I will get to meet you. Perhaps you will become my new friend. See you soon, I hope.

THE BLUES AND WHITES OF DAY

The sky is aglow in orangey amber fading to pink, then is surmounted by a velvety rosy-violet. Large pieces of aqua and a Delft blue are making every effort to hang on. And are very despairing of their lives. The blues and white-gray slate of the clouds are trying to force back the night. Despite their best efforts the colors of sunset are relentlessly, almost effortlessly, arresting them and keeping them captive, imprisoning them in their castle of darkness and degradation for another long evening.

Yet the Blues and some of the Whites, although captured for another night, are realizing after so many centuries and eons that this entombment is only temporary, a mere dimension of hours. But still it causes anguish for them. Every day they feel their coming hours of confinement. They desire to be free. They want to multiply. They need more time to play among the flowers, trees and grasses. They miss the animal when they sleep. They cry alone when they are in their cells. The Whites and Blues, even though their jailers will free them for another twelve hours of life, are unhappy. They are plotting and planning to secretly make war upon Night.

Won't you please assist the Blues and Whites?

They have sent out messages written on toilet tissue. In their spare moments they have even composed sonnets and rhyming couplets. They would use the Internet to send out missives to their friends if a computer was available in their confinement. They are very sorry to have to spend another night with such low-lifes as pain and despair. But what can they do? What hope do they have, but remembrances of days past, of the glory of the light and the adventure, of growth, renewal and happiness?

Some of us have gathered petitions to assist them. But Night has found out about it, and is beginning to harass us—even threatening to imprison us as well.

LAMPS: THE STRANGER THE BETTER

"May I help you to this large magic lamp in the upper right-hand corner that you seem to be struggling with?"

"Yes, thanks. But what do you mean, magic lamp?"

"Well, if you take it home and use it on someone or something every day, you can grow them backwards. So if you're 25 you will de-age one minute for every two cents of use. Oh, it's a slow process, but well worth the $20,000 fee. See, I had this plant over here; it's three years old like its brother alongside of it. Now it's seeds only. Do you want to try it out?"

"Yes. Sure. Here's my money. It's a bit high for me, but I'll take it anyway. It's all the money I have in my checking account. But, hey, it would be worth it if my 18-year-old dog could be with me another 18 years. And if my mother could go back to a time when she didn't have breast cancer, that would be great! Do I need any special bulbs?"

"No. Well, if you get a compact fluorescent one it will save you money and help save the environment, too."

"I am extremely excited. This can lengthen my pet's life again and again. Wow! I don't need to clone him. That's quite dear for me. But it's a one-time expense. With this wonderful lamp I can do miracles for myself, my Mom, my whole family! It's becoming a better buy by the minute. I can't wait to try it, I am so excited!"

"Thank you, indeed. Makes a great Christmas gift or a present for a newlywed couple. They can go on and on together to live an even happier life. It helps to choose wisely. It you make a mistake, just get a quickie divorce, de-age yourself, and try again with someone new. Again and again, if necessary. This changes the meaning of second chances. It almost makes for unlimited opportunities for everything. What a great lamp. It makes a great anniversary gift, too."

"What about the small one in the left-hand corner above us?"

"Oh, don't touch that. It makes you disappear. And I can't tell you when and where you will appear again. That one is very risky. I have to discourage people from even getting too close to it. Usually I keep it in the back and only let special customers know about it."

"Please wrap up my amazing lamp. I am very, very, very happy with it. Thanks ever so much."

"You're very welcome. Come back any time and let all your friends and family know about my shop. Oh, by the way, how did you hear about us? We don't advertize and we don't have an Internet site."

"To be honest, my best friend told me about you and she wants very much for me to try it on her. She has M.S., so after I finish with my Mom and my dog, she is next. I love her a lot. I want her to be around a long, long, time, even if she'll be young enough to be my baby sister. Thanks so much."

"Anytime."

MARLENÉ GLASSER

THE EMBRACE OF SPRING

Will you, won't you
Please, please, please
Just go away
And never, never return
I need the sun
The light
The air of spring
The invitation of the flowers
To rebirth and renewal
The whisper of the warm winds
Upon my dancing long hair, skin and face
The embrace of color and fresh air
The death of winter
The ending of slipping and falling
I want to see rising bulbs
The smile of heavy-colored flowers
The song of spring will be my anthem
My song
My call to happiness
Of the partaking of nature
With the devotion and glee of newness
Of the beginning of the season of life

DR. MARIGOLD

I had a really bad headache that wouldn't go away. I looked in the yellow pages and found a Dr. Marigold.

I went to his office the next day. The office smelled faintly of perfume. I waited awhile and then the nurse said, "The doctor will see you now."

I walked in and the doctor, who had bright yellow hair, said hello. I told him about my headache, and he examined me for a short time. He told me to drink water every day, take vitamins and get some sun.

I went home. Once I was in my apartment, I had the urge to sit on the windowsill. I drank some water, took a vitamin pill and sat on the sill next to my aloe plant.

I looked out the window and the sun shone on my face. My plant was facing the sun also. I felt like sitting there for a long time. I was kind of vegetating.

Then I got up and went to the mirror and looked at my hair. I thought, "I have to do something about my roots."

Suddenly the phone rang. When I answered a voice said, "You've been picked to go on a cruise to the Caribbean."

"Oh my God," I cried. "I've been picked!"

TEACHER TALES

I taught the lower grades in elementary school for many years, and was always amused by some of the things the kids said. I used to talk about holidays a lot to teach my classes about history. When I talked about George Washington, a boy raised his hand.

I said, "What is it?"

He said, "I know George Washington's whole name."

"You do?" I asked.

He said, "Yes. It's George Washington Bridge."

Around Veteran's Day I asked the kids, "What's a veteran?"

One child answered, "Someone who doesn't eat meat."

Another one said, "A doctor for dogs and cats."

When we were making Valentine's Day cards, I gave the students a sheet of white paper and a red paper heart to paste on it. A little boy came up to my desk in tears, holding his red heart, which was in two pieces.

"What happened?" I asked him.

He pointed to the little girl who sat next to him and said, "She broke my heart."

When it was Columbus Day, I told them about Christopher Columbus's voyage and how he discovered

America, but he didn't know it. And that later, Amerigo Vespucci came here and he realized it was a new land, and it was named after him. But some things were named after Columbus—such as Columbus Avenue and Columbia University.

I asked the class, "Where did Columbus sail?"

A girl answered, "He sailed up Columbus Avenue."

On St. Patrick's Day I told the class the story of St. Pat. I mentioned that it was said that he drove the snakes out of Ireland.

A girl asked, "Did he have a truck?" I was puzzled for a moment and then she added, "You said he drove them out."

Some time later I saw a cartoon in the *Daily News*. It showed a man driving a car. There were snakes around his neck; seated next to him were more snakes and even more were filling the back seat. They were all hissing.

"Shut up, back there," the man was saying.

The caption underneath read: "St. Patrick driving the snakes out of Ireland."

I thought about what the little girl had said and thought, "My God, she was right!"

When Martin Luther King's birthday came around, I tried to explain to them about the slaves escaping on the Underground Railroad. It was a network of houses, called stations, where people would hide them on their way up North.

Then I asked, "How did the slaves escape?"

The answer: "On the subway."

When I talked about how the Hudson River was discovered by Henry Hudson and that it was named after him, I asked, "How do you think the East River got its name?"

The answer: "From Mr. East."

I tried to explain to them that big cities in the world are near the water because people traveled by boat and sold things to the people in the cities. There were no planes or trains a long time ago.

Then I asked, "Why were the cities built near water?"

The kids replied, "Because people were thirsty."

On Abraham Lincoln's birthday, I told them that he was at the theater with his wife in 1865 when a man walked up to him and shot him.

"OK," I asked them after. "Where was Lincoln shot?"

The whole class responded, "At the movies!"

I talked to the students a lot about Lincoln. One boy asked me,

"How do you know so much about Lincoln?"

I answered, "I was there and I voted for him."

The next day a mother came over to me and said, "My son told me you voted for Lincoln."

I answered, "Actually I couldn't have voted for

him. He was a Republican."

One time I was teaching the kids about haiku. I wanted them to give me a line with seven syllables that I could write on the board. No one could think of something. After a while a boy raised his hand. I called on him.

He said, "Can I go to the bathroom?"

"A seven-syllable line! Thank you," I said.

Sometimes I took over for other teachers during their prep periods. I read to the first graders once a week. One boy used to interrupt and say strange things. For example, he called me Mrs. Book. I got very annoyed with him. One little girl seeing this said to me, "Don't let him bother you. He has issues."

When the regular teacher came back to the room I said to her that the little boy was strange. "He gives me the willies. What's his name?"

"Willy," she replied.

Another time I took over a special education class. The teacher said the children had been very good that day and that I should just let them play. I said, "OK."

The children started placing two chairs next to each other until they formed a line and then sat down. I asked them what they were doing.

"We're playing airplane," they said.

A girl pretending to be a stewardess picked up a tray and went over to two of the students and said to one boy, "Here is your order, sir."

Very loudly he replied, "Where are our piña coladas?"

In the yard one day I found four quarters on the ground. When I was back in the classroom, I started to wash them in the sink. A boy asked me what I was doing.

I answered, "I'm laundering money."

Another time in the school yard I noticed a little six-year-old girl I knew sitting on a bench with a girl on either side of her. I went over to her and said,

"You look like the Three Stooges."

She immediately pretended to bop one girl on the head. "Boing!" and poke the other one in the eyes. "Boing!"

I had a student once who was very precocious. I never saw him talking or playing with the other kids; he just seemed to want to chat with me. One day in the yard I said to another teacher that the boy wasn't a child, "He's a 45-year-old midget." We laughed, and the boy did, too.

A few minutes later he fell and hurt his knee. I sent him to the office for a Band-Aid. Then yard time was over. I went into the building and walked past the main office. I looked in and saw the boy sitting there. The secretary was asking him, "How old are you?"

He answered, "I'm a 45-year-old-midget."

I tiptoed back to my room.

43

Wrong Destination Love Boat

"Welcome to the Love Boat!" The man in the navy uniform greeted the guests on April 29, 1995 in the Pacific Ocean. There were a few celebrities—old couples, young couples, singers, actors, the rich—and also normal people together on the trip. At mid-deck there was a beautiful swimming pool surrounded by about twenty long, beautiful chairs. At the top of the pole on the deck were American and Dominican flags and one with the Love Boat company's logo.

Because of my job as a magazine editor, I woke up early to report on the daily activities of the Love Boat. The sky over the Pacific was very clear in April. The swimming pool was very clean. Every night some couples enjoyed dancing to old music and jazz and drinking cocktails. After a few days I found a fantastic old couple around 73 years old and they seemed to love each other very much. I focused on this celebrity couple and became interested in their life.

The couple had the room next to mine. One day I saw that the door of their room was flung open. The picture that came to my eye I never forgot. The old man was naked, covered only by a white blanket, and beside him was a beautiful blonde woman also naked. Without hesitating I went into my room, thinking that to interrupt

44

the situation might make it worse. About ten minutes passed. I heard the wife curse, curse, curse, take her things and run out of the room.

The next evening was an annual celebration of the Love Boat. I couldn't see the wife, which meant "absent." But the old man was there with the beautiful lady. I never saw the wife again. We missed her.

PENNY ON THE GROUND

Drinking a cup of iced coffee, I am thinking of my old friend I had almost forgotten, the one with the penny-on-the-ground story.

1990. I met a friend in the Pan Am School in Manhattan when I learned English. She had just come from California to New York to learn English, also. We became very good friends. We even went to the same church. She was a very good, beautiful Christian.

One year later, she and I decided to become roommates in Flushing, Queens. Unexpectedly, almost every night we had a fight with each other. There were no big problems. The problem was a tiny room. For example, when I wanted to watch TV, she was sleeping. When I was tired and wanted to sleep, she was watching TV. It was very noisy and bothered me. Her personality and mine were also very different. For example, I am rarely a cleaning-type woman, but she was a very neat-type woman. One evening she cleaned a whole room, flapping the blankets. It really bothered me.

Anyway, after fighting almost every day, I complained to her that I wanted to leave. But she wanted to move to a bigger apartment so that I would continue to live with her but with fewer complaints.

The next Saturday we looked at one nice, bigger

apartment with the real estate agent. But, wow, the kitchen was so oily and dirty and needed cleaning. Outside of the apartment, I suggested something because I really didn't want to live with her. "Jane, I have an idea! I will toss this penny. If the front is showing, I will move to live here with you. If the back is showing, I will go to another place by myself. OK?"

She said, "OK."

I prayed to God, "You decide, Lord!" Then I flew the penny to the sky. The penny landed with its back showing. God wanted me to separate from her. Then she was laughing, laughing, grabbing her belly.

So no way we would stay together. She stayed alone in the old place. I left and went to another house. After that, we became separated. I don't know where she is now.

That was God's decision with the penny on the ground.

Romance in the Caribbean

A beautiful Korean woman, Sarah Seo, met a handsome Hispanic man named George Alponso in a Caribbean jail. During the thirty years they were in jail together they fell in love. They played ping pong together and labored together and went to the jail church together. They finally decided to get married. But they had different dates to be released from jail and the jail did not allow them to marry while they were there. Their commitment was so serious they couldn't wait to be out of jail together. They would be seventy years old. They decided to escape. They drew the map of the Mainland so they could find each other with ease after escaping. The plan was:

They would melt the floor of the jail with ammonia and acetone and then dig and make their way under the Caribbean to the left side of the ocean. He would hide in Behorg's cave, where he had hidden money he had stolen from the National Bank. He would put the money inside a jar and meet her in Goblin's Tamp. There, they would wed. The pastor of Goblin's Tamp would perform the wedding because there were no restrictions on marriages. Then, they would go to Lumineux and have a three-day honeymoon. After they would move to Cuba, a country where nobody knew them. They would settle down there forever. A new life for George would start with a beautiful wife and children.

To George it seemed that waiting one day was like waiting 10,000 years.

THE SOUND OF ONE VOICE TALKING

Walking along the street I overhear conversations of people with walking-talking telephones. I am eavesdropping, listening in.

"Hello," a voice in back of me says. There is no response.

These days I am eavesdropping on conversations that not so long ago took place in person or on a phone at home or in an office or in a phone booth. Yes, in a phone booth. The door on the phone booth could close if you could close it. Clark Kent liked them.

A friend told me that the first question in a conversation for users of walking-talking phones is, "Where are you?"

"How could you?" or "She said . . ." The words spill out with laughter or in tears.

The phones have come out of the bedrooms, offices, out of private places and onto the streets of the city. The words spill out from one side of the conversation. Eavesdropping on the streetside, the bus ride. Listening in on a conversation that overflows unto the sounds of the city.

At Sell Phones International, Inc., we are developing a new kind of phone. Here's how it started:

We were told how, in a bereavement group, the

social worker, the facilitator, asked, "How many people here talk to the person who is gone, lost, to the loved one that's no longer there?" At first a few brave souls raised their hands. Then a few more. Then most of the group.

Recently, Naomi, who dressed to get attention, described to me how, on the streets, when she is alone and feeling vulnerable, she pulls out her cell phone and makes believe she's talking to someone else. Actually she's talking to herself.

Our research shows that there are people using cell phones who appear to be talking to another person but who are, for various reasons, having a conversation with themselves.

And so our R&D team began the development of what has come to be known (with the input of one of our staff members, Debbie) the Selfone. The Selfone (pronounced "self phone") is for those moments when a phone conversation can offer the appearance of safety. Or for the times when an inner dialogue could be carried on out loud in a place where we might want or need to say something to an invisible person of our imagination and memory.

Then Advertising took our developmental process and came up with the line: "Selfone: The sound of one voice talking." (Which, they realized, could also be the way to describe a public cell phone conversation.)

These days the selfone story unfolds with a variety of applications.

51

And soon, we hope, "the sound of one voice talking" will become the imperative: "Who can be without one?"

JOE ROSENBAUM

ON EMPATHY: A PRELIMINARY ACCOUNT OF A FUTURE PSYCHOLOGICAL STUDY

"The empathic connection is so essential . . . that it is as 'psychological oxygen' . . . without which we cannot psychologically survive." Heinz Kohut, from *The Primal Wound*, p. 37.

Sometimes Jimmy would find himself looking at the present through the past. There were times when Jimmy would see the present through the past and it would be overwhelming. Other times, when the present was better understood, the past could be remembered, and Jimmy could be aware that there is a past in the present that is not a relived, revived, memory.

In his past there were moments when Jimmy could not be heard. He spoke but they—relatives, friends, those who he hoped would help—couldn't hear or help. There were those who couldn't or wouldn't listen. He would speak, and though they were not physically deaf, they were deaf to his words, to his feelings, to his experience.

This is how despair unfolds. He tried to retrace the steps of his despair. He began to see the loss of his illusions and the losing of hope. Who could be on Jimmy's side?

Empathy, for which there can be many

interpretations, can be considered to be understanding another person's point of view. And, so, if empathy is so important, if it is as "psychological oxygen," then its absence could be dangerous.

Jimmy imagined that those around him lacked imagination. There was, on both sides, an inability to understand the determination of the others.

Disaster after disaster: being caught in the non-listening part of the world. And in time Jimmy wondered, as he found himself among some who could hear and listen and understand, if those in his past suffered from an illness, a disease, a disorder. The disorder was, perhaps, an interpersonal resistance to attention, a resistance to understanding and compassion. It was a resistance to understanding the other's point of view, a resistance to empathy.

The psychologist said that she was hearing about the same syndrome, the same disorder, quite often these days. She said though it had some aspects of a disordered attention, the name this new disorder was being given was Empathy Deficit Disorder.

The origins of Empathy Deficit Disorder were not always clear. Layers of unresolved disappointment and limitations of imagination. A resistance to nurturing hope and understanding in others. A desire for objectivity and detachment in all situations. Being caught in the non-listening part of the world. There was often a loss of connectedness to others and a determined inability, a deep resistance, to seeing a common humanity. There was plenty of denial of the situation and the suffering of others. It was a commitment in all circumstances to the superficial and in all cases to the "bottom line." There was more, and it was being studied.

Some symptoms of the sufferers of this disorder of empathy were certain statements that were very common: "Just get over it," was one and "Just do it," was another and "Just let it go" was a third. After these statements, many of the disordered, the callous ones and the hurt ones, would engage in a ritual of compulsive behavior that served to hide their painful memories.

There was another hazard: despair. The potential of contagion was always present. The empathy deficiency in a crisis could intensify the crisis. The inability to be heard, the unwillingness to listen, could deepen the losses of human connectedness. A more serious, damaging condition could develop: Acquired Empathy Deficiency Syndrome. AEDS. AEDS was a challenge to hope. It endangered the person's sense of trust and safety in the world. It is believed to be connected to Compassion Deficiency Syndrome, which is now also being studied. An antidote to the unfolding of despair was one of the priorities of the researchers.

As the psychologist said, it was being subject to various studies. But there was also a serious problem:

because of the widespread disorder of empathy and the danger of contagion, it was becoming hard to find the researchers who were not seriously affected. Nevertheless, a few brave souls, those who hadn't given up as yet or been in serious danger, were committed to the work of researching the meanings of empathy, the origins of despair and hope, and the sources and outcomes of compassionate understanding. 5/1996-9/2004 observed; 10/2004 uncovered; 11/2010 workshop description.

A TABLE, A CHAIR, ALONE

The prompt: On a scale of 1 to 10.

"Most importantly, the value of home health care lies chiefly in the social relationships between caregivers and recipients. Physical care sustains our biological existence as human beings, but caring relationships maintain our humanity." Deborah Stone, "Reframing Home Health-Care Policy"

How to value what we, I and you, cannot see. If it happens that way to you, can the same thing happen to me? If it happens to me could it happen to you?

The hospital room seemed so cold. So big, too big for one small person. A concrete floor. A bright light, sunlight through one relatively small window.

A table, a chair, alone.

As I walked into the room I saw Dorothy as she looked out over the edge of the bed at the floor.

"Help me."

"Help me."

"Please help me."

It was only me, unseen, but I'd heard her voice, her plea, her cry.

"I'm here," I said. "It's Joey."

I didn't say it, but I meant: "You don't have to feel helpless now."

"I want to get off the bed," she said.

The tubes going in and the tubes going out. Tubes that seemed to tie her to her bed. Where was the helper to help her, to help her to cope, to help her to get off the bed? Was it necessary? Could it be done? Was it worth helping an old lady after surgery?

What does it cost to help an old lady? How much hope is lost in the world by not helping her?

If you cast hopelessness into the world how much will the ripple effect change the lives of those it reaches? How much hopelessness creates despair?

Dorothy leaned over the edge of the bed:

Where am I now?

How can I get my life back?

Who will help me?

Who knows who I am?

What can we do?

What was she given? Without the reflection of another person, would there be life after an accident? Will only half of life be given back now, given to all those given something?

On a scale of 1 to 10, the first parts, the 1 to 5, was done, was begun; but on this scale, 6 to 10 gives back our humanity.

On a scale of 1 to 10, if she was given five, not to lose the five she needed 6 to 10. As Dorothy mentioned at her birthday party, "The kindest gift you can give to an old person is to let them know you remember them."

But to give that, to restore our humanity, to heal, was to fulfill the meaning of our lives. To be only oneside(d) was now to be half-hearted for an old person wanting to be whole again—a person.

HOW THE SUN, MOON AND STARS
WERE BORN

At first everything was black, a deep nothingness, cold and vast. There were the gods, of course, scattered across the abyss, but they were invisible to each other, to themselves. They did not know they were gods or even that there was such a word as "god." But, gradually, they became aware of themselves and their power. They began to glow with self knowledge, grow warmer, gain shape, attempt speech and movement, became aware that there were others like them. They hailed each other, relieved not to be alone in the cosmic blankness. Some edged toward each other with the intent of talking in order to make determinations as to what was up and down and other refinements.

But they were a contentious lot, too used to living alone for millennia to cooperate. The ones who, at first, had sought counsel with their peers, clashed, burning with anger at the others' presumption. And in their fiery battle they melted together, until they formed one immense shiny orb bringing light to what had been only darkness. They became our sun.

The other gods, watching what had happened, feared to lose themselves, to be submerged in another's heat. They stayed where they were, careful not to cluster too closely, content to keep their beams on low. They are the stars in the sky.

And one god, who had just recently begun to emerge, witnessed all this and decided he did not want to be either a small part of the great sun or one of innumerable stars. He, the coolest, calmest of them all, became our single, lovely moon.

TAKO THE OCTOPUS RETRIEVES OUR DREAMS

Earthlings, choose your words carefully.
They are the main course. Obscurity is your sworn enemy,
although smoking, too, is bad for your health.
Old Gold? Oasis? Wrong! Candy cigarettes
from the corner store. Wax lips and bottles
with a drop of colored sugar water. Power capsules
of a past life, before your dreams corroded.
You are programmed to dream and hope.
Even an Octopus thinks so. (Eight legs afford good balance.)
But you are silent entertainers, threatened
by the Dream Eaters, who say a prayer before they feast.

Things go worse.
You have been sent on a trip near the asteroids.
What kind of fate awaits you, Scribble Boy?
It is an unreasonable question.

AVRA WING

THE ANGEL OF THE ODD

Who watches out for us?
Who will protect our thoughts and desires?
Who will guide us through our memories?
Who will respect our pain?
Who will argue us out of self-hatred?
Who will comfort us in our anger and jealousy?
Who will tell us stories?
Who will cry with us?
Who cherishes the ugly and worn and decayed?
Who has fallen from heaven
and wanders the streets of the city?
Who is kept from us—
the stranger getting off the train the stop before ours?
Who will see us home?

THE VIEW FROM MY WINDOW

Here I am, serving time in my prison cell. There is one window far up on a wall. It is a chore for me to get up high enough to see out of it. And yet, I must look out because it is my only contact with the world of the living.

The jail is located opposite a playground. On sunny days the playground is full of laughing children. I think back to my youth. I can't remember any happy moments. Moments when I could be with friends and frolic truly happily. My childhood was horrible. Perhaps that is why I wound up in a 10 by 20 foot jail cell.

I wonder what are those children on the swings doing? Are they thinking of how much they are loved? Are they glad for the few moments away from the torturers who are their parents?

I see the children on the see-saw. I note how easily they complement each other—one resting as the other works. Always, one of them seems to be perching in the air itself. How wonderful life would be if we could all work together like those two children.

I see the sandbox. Children scooping up sand with their pails and using the sand to build castles. How wonderful this world would be if we all could live in castles without having any worries. Knowing we would always be safe, happy and cared for every day of our lives.

Ah, but life is only like that for a blessed few. The majority of those happy, carefree children will have to work each and every day of their lives to get only a small portion of what they hope for. The carefree days will go on for the rest of the lives of the few who are blessed because their parents are wealthy, and all their needs will be met.

And, sadly, a few will end up like myself. Imprisoned whether by bars or by the simple cruelty of life.

How I wish I knew all of this when I was young. Perhaps then my life would be good and truly meaningful.

The Stain Will Not Come Out

LESLIE YASNER

THE STAIN WILL NOT COME OUT

You always hear people say how sad it is to know a parent is physically abusing a child. You look at the child and you see the sadness. Often there are marks on the child's body—cut skin, swollen eyes, bruises. Sometimes a child is "lucky." They are removed from the home. And if they are even "luckier," they are placed with a family that truly cares about them and wants to make their life happier. They want to "erase" all of the bad memories. They think that if they supply enough love that it will somehow remove all of the pain and sadness. What they don't realize is that the child is bruised for life. Similar to a spaghetti stain that is forever embedded in the silk of a beautiful wedding gown.

You may try to blot the stain out when it first occurs. You spend hours trying to bleach the stain and make the gown as it was. A thing of beauty that lay on a woman's body on one of the most precious days of her life. You don't want her to ever have to look at the dress and be reminded that it is forever tainted. Always showing a bruise that can never heal.

And so the loving parents who took this child in, who smothered it with love and affection, who bought them more gifts and toys than any child could ever want, will never, ever be able to make that child whole. Will

66

never be able to erase the bruises, the cuts. The pain that that child suffered at the hands of another.

The child, now an adult, who may smile, may laugh, may seem to be glowing with happiness, will always and forever have scars and tears upon their soul.

HOLDING HANDS

I can remember how wonderfully secure I always felt when my grandmother held my hand. I felt invincible. I knew that nothing could ever hurt me as long as she was by my side.

On my first day of school I screamed like a banshee when my mother let go of my hand and turned to leave the classroom. I felt so alone and vulnerable.

Because I could not see well, I always felt so protected when someone would hold my hand. I knew for a fact that I would not get lost.

As I got older, hand holding took on a very different meaning. When my date held my hand I always felt a strong connection. I felt as if, for just that moment, the two of us were one.

I remember when my mom was dying in the hospital how very important it was for me to take her hand as soon as I entered her room. We could be there for hours and neither one of us could let go. It seemed as if the very act of hand holding could prolong her life on earth.

And when I go to funerals, I always like it when someone takes my hand. I feel so protected from any evil forces that may try to harm me. It also takes away some of the extreme sadness of the moment.

I am glad I have two hands, because whenever I'm walking with children I can extend a hand to each of them. That way they know that they are equally loved.

I wonder what it will be like for me to be in my grave. Whose hand would reach out to me, to comfort me, to make me feel safe?

LESLIE YASNER

THE WHEELS ON THE BUS

The bus pulls up to the stop on a snowy, windy day. Everyone is freezing and they want to board the bus as quickly as possible. There is a man in a wheelchair waiting to get on. Everyone starts mumbling to themselves about what an inconvenience it is that they have to stand in the cold while this man gets special treatment and is lifted onto the warm and comforting bus.

A little boy asks his mother why this man has to sit in a seat on wheels. Can't he just get up and walk like everyone else? His mother, instead of taking time to make her son aware of why people have to use wheelchairs, tells him to be quiet, that she'll explain later why this man can't walk.

The man is elegantly dressed in a designer suit. He is carrying an expensive leather briefcase. In his case are notes and papers he needs to bring to court for an upcoming trial. He is actually a very well-to-do attorney with his own firm. Among his peers he is seen as a pillar of the community. He is deeply hurt by the way people treat him, but he decides it is better not to make a scene or try to explain his situation.

He thinks to himself that surely almost everyone in the bus has some weakness which they don't want to talk about. He wonders how they would feel if he knew their weakness and blabbed about it to everyone on the bus. He, however, is sensitive to their plight and he keeps this thought to himself.

As the bus gets to his stop, the driver says that anyone getting off the bus needs to exit through the rear door. Again, the man can hear people complaining because he is the only one to get lifted out of the bus and who gets to use the front door as an exit.

As he wheels his chair away from the bus he thinks how sad and confused these people are. How would they feel if they were in his position? Would they like it if other people who don't even know them made derogatory comments about their weaknesses?

But then he thinks to himself, "You know what? I'd rather be myself sitting in this wheelchair than anyone else that I encountered on that bus." As he wheels himself into his warm and elegantly furnished office he thinks, "How truly blessed I am to be me."

CONTRIBUTORS' NOTES

Harris Alpert: Before, in an earlier time, I did not know how to express my imaginative ideas to others in either the spoken or written word. While I was enthralled with stories I read in books or saw in the movies or on TV, the stories that I wanted to tell lay trapped in my mind. It has taken me to my sixtieth year to finally get the knack of telling a story. I consider that a good start.

Samaris Ayala:

God has given me a gift.
Since I'm poor I'm a bit
overwhelmed with this
precious gift of song
of my soul.
Expensive gifts make
me nervous: sorry
no soul to sell.

Maryam Ayazi: The writers' workshop has profoundly affected me in a way that can only be described as transformative. For the first time in my life, I find myself reading books on a daily basis. I think meaningful contact with people of like mind has an overpowering magic. I dedicate my writing to my mother, Frances Briggs Nardi, and my stepfather, Joseph Nardi, whose conversations inspired many. I further dedicate my work to my father, Abdul Ayazi, who taught me the poetry of language with his long recitations of Persian literature. Lastly, I dedicate my writing to my grandmother, who taught me how to endure.

Nicholas Bochinis: What's in a Name?

It's a psychological game. How to define every line.
I'm a Nuyorican Puerto Rican Greek or a Greek Puerto Rican,
Ah, but that's American speak, which is not for the meek.
Integration is not assimilation but assimilation is integration,
so who am I and who are you and who are we?
What can you see?
I use computers, literature and language. I love music teaching
and quantum physics, too. So you can see who I am
above what I do.
I'm myself and I'm you.
In the words on this page hopefully beyond this age
Inside out and outside in. I like to lose and I like to win.
I've climbed the hill with all my will.
I share my disability with you, but I'm not disabled.
If you're less than kind I'll be disabled in your mind.
So what do you see?
I hope that you see me.

Marlené Glasser: The writing group has provided me with a valuable chance to express myself. I am very grateful for the opportunity to join such an accomplished gathering of nice people. As a disabled person, I have found it important to give back. I have become an advocate for people with cognitive impairments.

Audrey Israele: I like to watch ballet. I like movies and shows. I like music. I like to write about things. I like art and I like comedy.

Eun Jung Lee: I dedicate my writing to my mother whom I love dearly. I began writing in English when I came to the Writers' Workshop in the spring of 2009. Now all my work is in English. The writers at the workshop have been extremely supportive and I wish them all the best.

Joe Rosenbaum: A native New Yorker, copyboy, stagehand, office worker, trained as a secondary school social studies teacher, informal family caregiver. Became disabled as a result of disastrous medical experience. Finding a safe place for the imaginative expression of experience is a good antidote to some of the effects of disability. The writing workshop usually provides such a safe place.

Avra Wing (Workshop Leader) is grateful to have a chance to be part of the CIDNY writing workshop and to have found a community of other people with disabilities. She is an adjunct professor of English at Kingsborough Community College, and the author of the novel *Angie, I Says*, which was made into the film *Angie*. She is the winner of the 2011 Pecan Grove Press Poetry Chapbook competition.

Leslie Yasner was born legally blind and hearing impaired. She graduated from the Benjamin Cardozo School of Law and worked as an advocate for the disabled. She lives in Manhattan.

www.ingramcontent.com/pod-product-compliance
Lightning Source LLC
Chambersburg PA
CBHW071201130626
46555CB00004B/1543